AF598995

COMING TOGETHER ON 9/11

BY SUSAN E. HAMEN

childsworld.com

Published by The Child's World®
800-599-READ • www.childsworld.com

Photography Credits
Photographs ©: Joe Robbins/AP Images, cover, 1; Eric Draper/George W. Bush Presidential Library/American Photo Archive/Alamy, 5; Red Line Editorial, 6, 26; Doug Mills/AP Images, 8; Gordon Wheaton/Shutterstock Images, 9; Alan Budman/Shutterstock Images, 11; Bastiaan Slabbers/iStockphoto, 12; Eric Draper/National Archives, 14; iStockphoto, 16, 17; Tamer A. Soliman/Shutterstock Images, 18; Doug Kanter/AFP/Getty Images, 21; Beth Keiser/STF/AP Images, 22; Paul Morse/National Archives, 24; Drew Angerer/Getty Images News/Getty Images, 27; Spencer Platt/Getty Images News/Getty Images, 28

ISBN Information
9781503889149 (Reinforced Library Binding)
9781503890855 (Portable Document Format)
9781503892095 (Online Multi-user eBook)
9781503893337 (Electronic Publication)

LCCN 2023950400

Printed in the United States of America

ABOUT THE AUTHOR

Susan E. Hamen has written many books for young readers. She lives in Minnesota with her husband and two children. Like most Americans her age and older, she remembers exactly where she was on the morning of the 9/11 attacks. She had just gotten into her car to go to work. She turned on the radio and sat in disbelief at what she heard.

CONTENTS

FAST FACTS

- On September 11, 2001, **terrorists** launched an attack on the United States. They **hijacked** four airplanes and planned to crash them into important buildings.
- When US airspace closed, hundreds of planes were left with nowhere to go. The people of Gander, Newfoundland, Canada opened their doors to thousands of people stranded in the town when their flights were forced to land there.
- In the days after the attacks, people around the country and world came together for **vigils** to honor the victims and find comfort.
- People around the United States donated blood to send to victims of the attacks. First responders came from all over to help with rescue efforts, and chefs and other volunteers stepped up to feed them.
- Because the terrorists behind 9/11 were Islamic extremists, people falsely blamed all Muslims for the attacks. Muslim Americans worked hard to fight **Islamophobia**.

President George W. Bush visited the World Trade Center attack site on September 14, 2001.

FANON

GREENLAND
ICELAND
Newfoundland
and
Labrador
Hudson
Bay
Gander
CANADA
New York
New York City
ATLANTIC
OCEAN
UNITED STATES
OF AMERICA
MEXICO
Gulf of Mexico
THE BAHAMAS
CUBA

CHAPTER ONE

THE HOSPITALITY OF GANDER

On the morning of September 11, 2001, the people of Gander, Newfoundland, Canada, woke up to what they thought would be a typical day. The small town of almost 10,000 people is on the island of Newfoundland. During World War II (1939–1945), the Gander airport was an important refueling stop for flights to and from Europe. But as technology improved, planes did not need to refuel to make the trip. The airport was still helpful for emergencies, but it saw more cargo than passengers. On September 11, though, the Gander airport would become busier than it had been in years. The people of Gander would play host to thousands of unexpected visitors.

More than 1,000 miles to the southwest, people in New York City also expected a normal morning. They made their way to work and school. But then tragedy struck.

The Gander airport was an important stop between Europe and Cuba from the mid to late 1900s. Cuban aircraft were not allowed to land in the United States.

President Bush was visiting an elementary school in Florida when he learned about the terrorist attacks.

At 8:46 a.m., a hijacked airplane crashed into the North Tower of the World Trade Center in Manhattan. At 9:03 a.m., another airplane struck the South Tower. Thousands of people were inside the towers. Terrorists from an organization known as al-Qaeda had overtaken the planes. Emergency crews responded immediately. The towers eventually collapsed. Terrorists also hit the Pentagon near Washington, DC. Another plane was heading for Washington, DC, when its passengers fought the terrorists. The plane crashed in a field near Shanksville, Pennsylvania. White House Chief of Staff Andrew Card told President George W. Bush, "America is under attack."

Canadian leaders were worried about security at airports in big cities. This is part of why small cities such as Gander ended up hosting planes.

Almost immediately, airspace over the United States was closed. All flights in the air were ordered to land. No aircraft were allowed into US airspace from other countries. Many planes were coming from overseas. If they had enough fuel to return to their starting airport, the planes were sent back. But some did not have the fuel. They needed a place to land. Canadian leaders closed Canada's airspace, too. But they allowed planes from overseas to land first. As part of Canada's Operation Yellow Ribbon, air traffic controllers worked in a frenzy to find alternate landing spots for inbound flights. Almost 250 flights were forced to land in Canada on September 11, 2001. Gander was one of 17 Canadian airports where planes landed.

A total of 38 planes landed in Gander. People from all over the world were on board. For many hours, the passengers were not allowed to leave the planes. As passengers and crew heard the news of the horrific attacks, they sat in shock. How would they get home? Where would they stay? Gander had very few hotels and restaurants. Fortunately, the local people had a plan for the unexpected visitors.

"Lend a hand, do what you can," the local television stations said. Schools and businesses closed so people from Gander and the surrounding towns could volunteer to help the stranded travelers. These travelers became known as the "plane people." School buses picked up approximately 7,000 plane people from the airport. The buses took them to local churches, schools, legion halls, and even homes. Temporary places to sleep had been set up all over town.

Residents cooked hot meals and gathered blankets for their guests. Public telephones were set up for the passengers to use to call loved ones. Local pharmacies made sure everyone had the prescriptions they needed for free. As food flowed in, the problem of storing it became an issue. The quick-thinking people of Gander solved that by using the local ice rink. Gander mayor Claude Elliott called it the nation's largest walk-in freezer.

The Broadway musical *Come From Away* tells the story of Gander on September 11, 2001.

When their guests were fed and sheltered, the people of Gander once again pulled together to offer their visitors some entertainment. Local bands put on concerts. Bowling matches were set up. Local cooks offered the stranded visitors a taste of local cooking, including dishes such as stewed moose.

On September 13, the first planes were allowed to leave Gander. The stranded visitors were able to return to their homes. But they would never forget the generosity and hospitality of the people of Gander. Many stayed in touch with their hosts. They felt the generosity of Gander was extraordinary. But, as Gander local Janice Goudie explained, "You don't turn your backs on people in need."

CHAPTER TWO

ORGANIZING VIGILS

The terrorist attacks on 9/11 killed 2,977 people. An estimated 2,753 people died at the World Trade Center in New York City. Twenty-three of the victims were New York police officers, and 343 were firefighters and paramedics who responded to the emergency. The Pentagon attack killed 125 people in the building.

More than 20 years after the September 11 attacks, people organize vigils in remembrance.

There were also 64 people onboard the plane. Another 40 victims on United Airlines Flight 93 lost their lives in Shanksville, Pennsylvania. September 11 was the single largest loss of life from a foreign attack on American soil. It was also the greatest loss of police officers, firefighters, and paramedics in a single day.

In the days that followed, Americans worried more attacks might be coming. Televisions, radios, and internet sites replayed footage and audio clips of the attacks. News programs provided continuous coverage as crews dug through the rubble looking for survivors. The nation struggled to make sense of the horrific attacks. President George W. Bush declared September 14 would be a National Day of Prayer and Remembrance. On September 13, he issued a proclamation stating, "I ask that the people of the United States and places of worship mark this National Day of Prayer and Remembrance with noontime memorial services, the ringing of bells at that hour, and evening candlelight remembrance vigils. I encourage employers to permit their workers time off during the lunch hour to attend the noontime services to pray for our land."

Current and former presidents and first ladies attended the National Day of Prayer and Remembrance service.

The following day, President Bush joined four former US presidents and other political figures at the Washington National Cathedral. Religious leaders of different faiths came together and spoke. A Roman Catholic archbishop from Washington led the congregation in prayer. His nephew, a firefighter, was still missing in the remains of the World Trade Center. A Muslim imam offered prayers and read from the Koran.

A Jewish rabbi called for peace throughout the country. A Christian minister delivered the sermon. Those in attendance listened as the interfaith speakers called on the nation to pray and remember those who were lost. The congregation sang "America the Beautiful" and other patriotic songs.

Similar services and vigils took place throughout the country. Nearly 15,000 people flooded into the City Hall Plaza in Boston, Massachusetts, for an interfaith prayer vigil. Muslim, Jewish, and Christian leaders led the crowd in prayers and songs. Rabbi Barry Starr urged the crowd to not turn to hate and revenge. "What we must fear most is not evil, it is becoming evil ourselves," he cautioned.

In Chicago, Illinois, several thousand people gathered at the Daley Center Plaza. A bell at the nearby First United Methodist Church rang as people held back tears. Large and small groups gathered throughout Chicago. Lana Layne attended one of these memorials. She said, "I'm here to feel with everyone else."

Boeing workers worldwide bowed their heads to observe a moment of silence for the three colleagues they had lost on Flight 77, which had flown into the Pentagon. Meanwhile, residents in Phoenix, Arizona, gathered for an interfaith prayer service at Patriots Square. Crowds gathered near Centennial Park's Parthenon statue in Nashville, Tennessee.

People hung posters for their missing loved ones around New York City. These became makeshift memorials for victims of the attacks.

The urge to mourn alongside others brought people together throughout New York City, across the country, and around the world. People gathered in places of worship, parks, town halls, and college campuses to pay tribute to those who had died. Peggy Lukas attended a gathering in Chicago. She said, "I didn't know what to do, so I just wanted to come out and in solidarity against terrorism and in unity as an American."

People around the country sent words of encouragement to New York City.

TO NEW YORK CITY
AND ALL THE RESCUERS:
KEEP YOUR SPIRITS UP...
OKLAHOMA LOVES YOU!!

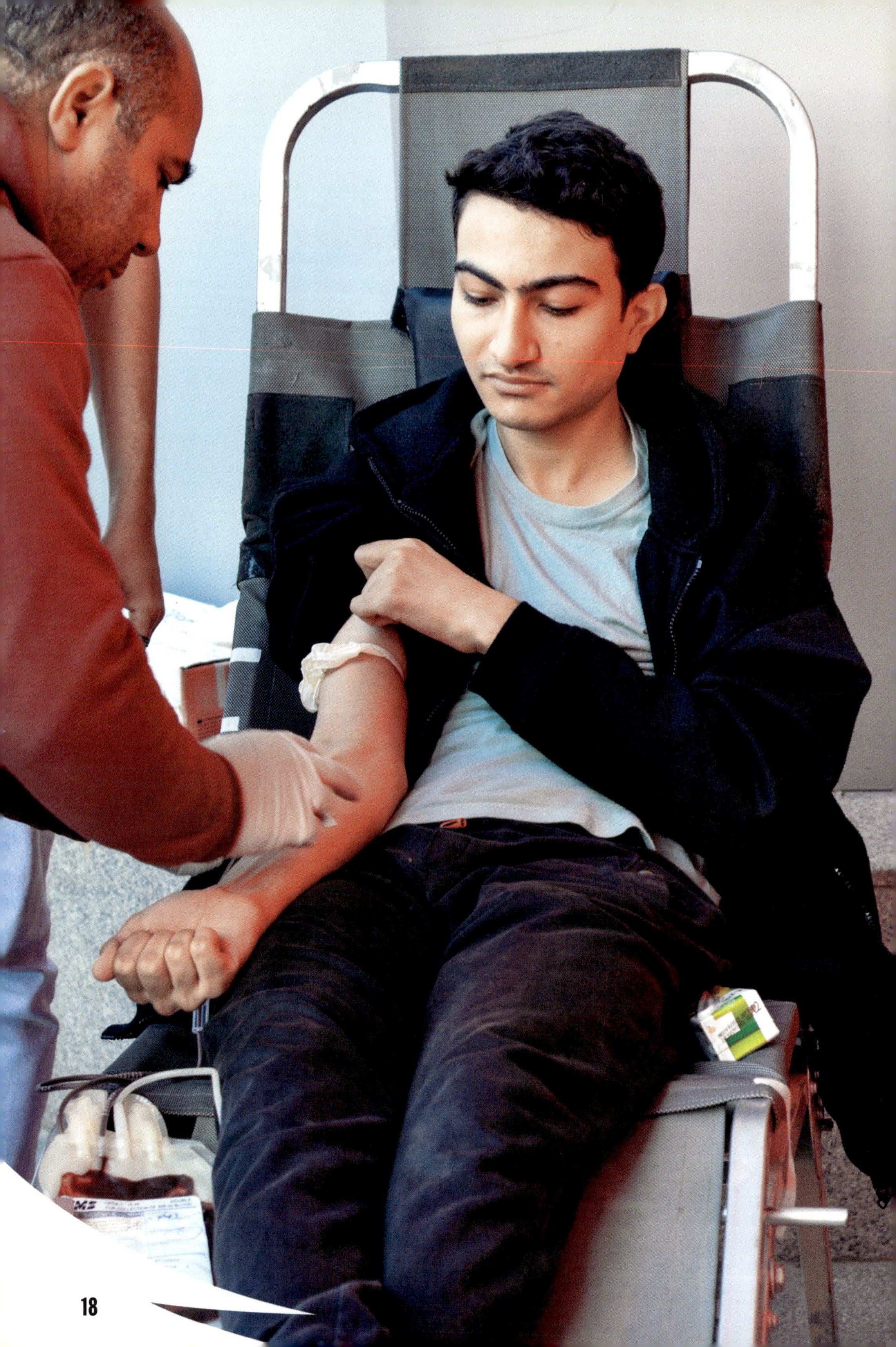

CHAPTER THREE

BLOOD DONATION AND FOOD DRIVES

Immediately following the September 11 attacks, medical professionals scrambled to help those who were injured. Serious injuries can cause victims to lose a lot of blood. Blood donation becomes crucial in times of disaster. Healthy people can donate blood. The blood is given to people who need it. People usually donate around 1 pint (.5 L), or one unit, of blood. The American Red Cross sent out urgent pleas for blood donations after 9/11. People around the country rushed to donate.

Beth Ann Ley worked at the San Diego Blood Bank. When she came to work on September 11, 2001, a line of people had wrapped around the building. "The response was overwhelming," she said. "It just made me really proud to work here." San Diego residents donated 380 units of blood that day. Another 4,000 people gave blood in the days that followed.

Blood donors must meet different requirements to givc blood. Donors can glve blood every two to four months, depending on the type of donation.

In the first two days following the attack, people nationwide donated 1.5 million units of blood. Only a small percentage of the blood ended up being needed. But the American Red Cross was overwhelmed by the number of people across the nation who were willing to help.

New York needed more than blood donations. Nearly 1.8 million tons (1.6 million m tons) of wreckage lay where the Twin Towers had once stood. Officially, the site was called Ground Zero. Rescue workers called it "the pile." Fires inside the rubble burned for more than 100 days, and cleanup efforts would take more than nine months. Rescue workers, firefighters, emergency medical technicians (EMTs), and others were trying to find survivors. Emergency workers came from all over the country to help. Some even came from Canada. Feeding so many workers became a challenge. But people were eager to step up and help.

Nino's Restaurant was eight blocks from the World Trade Center site. On September 12, the restaurant began offering free meals to workers. Nick Pasculli was the general manager. "We figured we'd feed 150 people," he said. But by November, the restaurant was serving up to 7,000 meals a day. The restaurant had served more than 500,000 meals to workers by June. People from all over donated food and volunteered to serve meals.

Nino's Restaurant served free meals to people involved in the rescue and cleanup effort at the World Trade Center.

NINO
We Will Stand Together
And Become Even Stronger
God Bless America

U.S.A.
IRON WORKERS

Ruth Reichl was the editor of the food magazine *Gourmet*. After the attacks, she asked her staff to meet at the magazine's test kitchens. Employees and their families arrived with groceries. They cooked and baked food for the workers. Then they delivered it straight to workers at Ground Zero. "We were attempting to snatch hope from the rubble of our broken city," Reichl explained. "And food was the perfect way to do it."

For many Americans, helping the rescue and recovery efforts meant offering aid in other ways. People of different ages, backgrounds, and abilities did whatever they could to send help. Many donated money to disaster relief organizations such as the American Red Cross. In addition to blood drives, this organization helps provide food, shelter, and other assistance after disasters. Some founded charities to help victims' families, as well as the survivors. September 11 is now the National Day of Service and Remembrance. More than 20 years after the attacks, people volunteer in their communities to honor the victims.

Lisa Poseley spent nine months volunteering after the September 11 attacks. She ran the Hard Hat Café, serving coffee and packaged foods to cleanup workers.

CHAPTER FOUR

FIGHTING ISLAMOPHOBIA

Not everyone came together in positive ways after 9/11. Hate crimes against Muslims greatly increased. A hate crime is a crime committed based on the victim's race or ethnicity, gender, or religion. The Council on American-Islamic Relations (CAIR) fights for **civil rights** for American Muslims.

President Bush spoke out against anti-Muslim attacks at the Islamic Center of Washington, DC, on September 17, 2001.

Because al-Qaeda was a terrorist organization of Muslim extremists, many Americans believed all Muslims were to blame for the attacks. In the days after 9/11, CAIR received numerous reports of hate crimes. These included threats and violence. Some people were fired from their jobs without reason. President Bush and the director of the FBI **condemned** these hate crimes. But life still changed for countless Muslim Americans after 9/11. In the years since, many Muslims have worked hard to change negative views of Islam. Some have run for political office to lead change across the nation. Others found work helping Muslims who have faced **discrimination**.

Qasim Rashid is Pakistani American. He was at work when the World Trade Center towers collapsed. He watched with some coworkers, shocked by what he saw. Then he heard a colleague whisper an anti-Muslim **slur**. He became afraid. “I was 19, Muslim, and I had a beard, and suddenly people couldn’t see me as American,” Rashid said. He wanted to help other people who had been mistreated. He became a human rights lawyer. He represents Muslims and other **marginalized** communities. “There have been immense atrocities and horrific violence committed against Muslims because of 9/11,” Rashid said.

"I knew I had to do something to create the kind of country I thought America should be."

Ruwa Romman was only eight years old on 9/11. She and her family had just immigrated to the United States. Romman faced daily bullying for the rest of elementary school. When Romman was in high school, a teacher pulled her out of class. The teacher asked if her family were terrorists. A close friend's parents banned Romman from their home because of her faith.

ANTI-ISLAMIC HATE CRIMES

The Federal Bureau of Investigation (FBI) began collecting information about hate crimes after the Hate Crime Statistics Act of 1990. Not all law enforcement organizations participate, and not all hate crimes are reported to police.

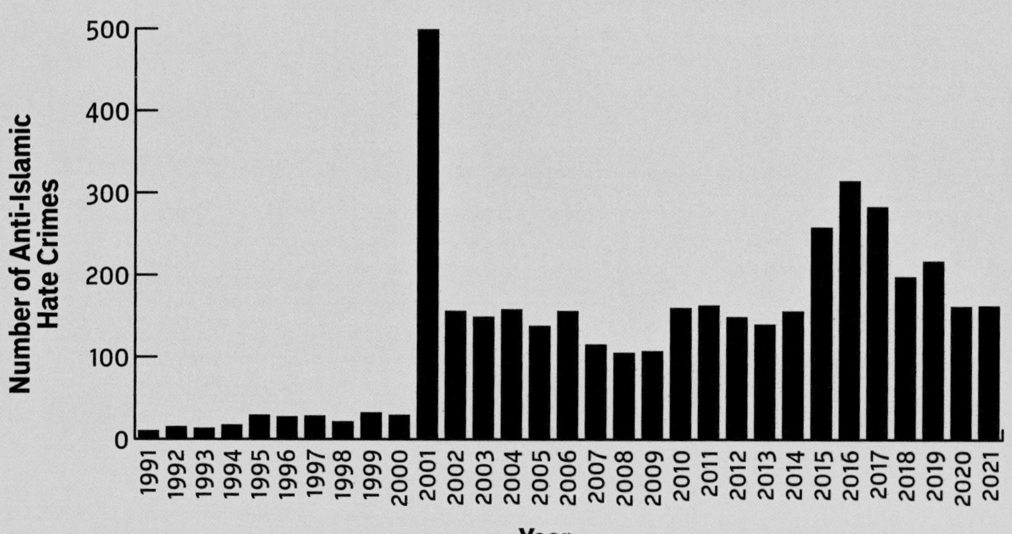

▲ Ilhan Omar (left) and Rashida Tlaib (right) became the first Muslim women elected to US Congress in 2018.

Romman and her family faced extra security screenings while traveling. Romman knew what had happened to her was wrong. "I remember trying so hard to get people to just see me as a person," she said. She wanted to **advocate** for her community and educate people. Romman became the communications director for CAIR in 2016. She continues to fight against Islamophobia.

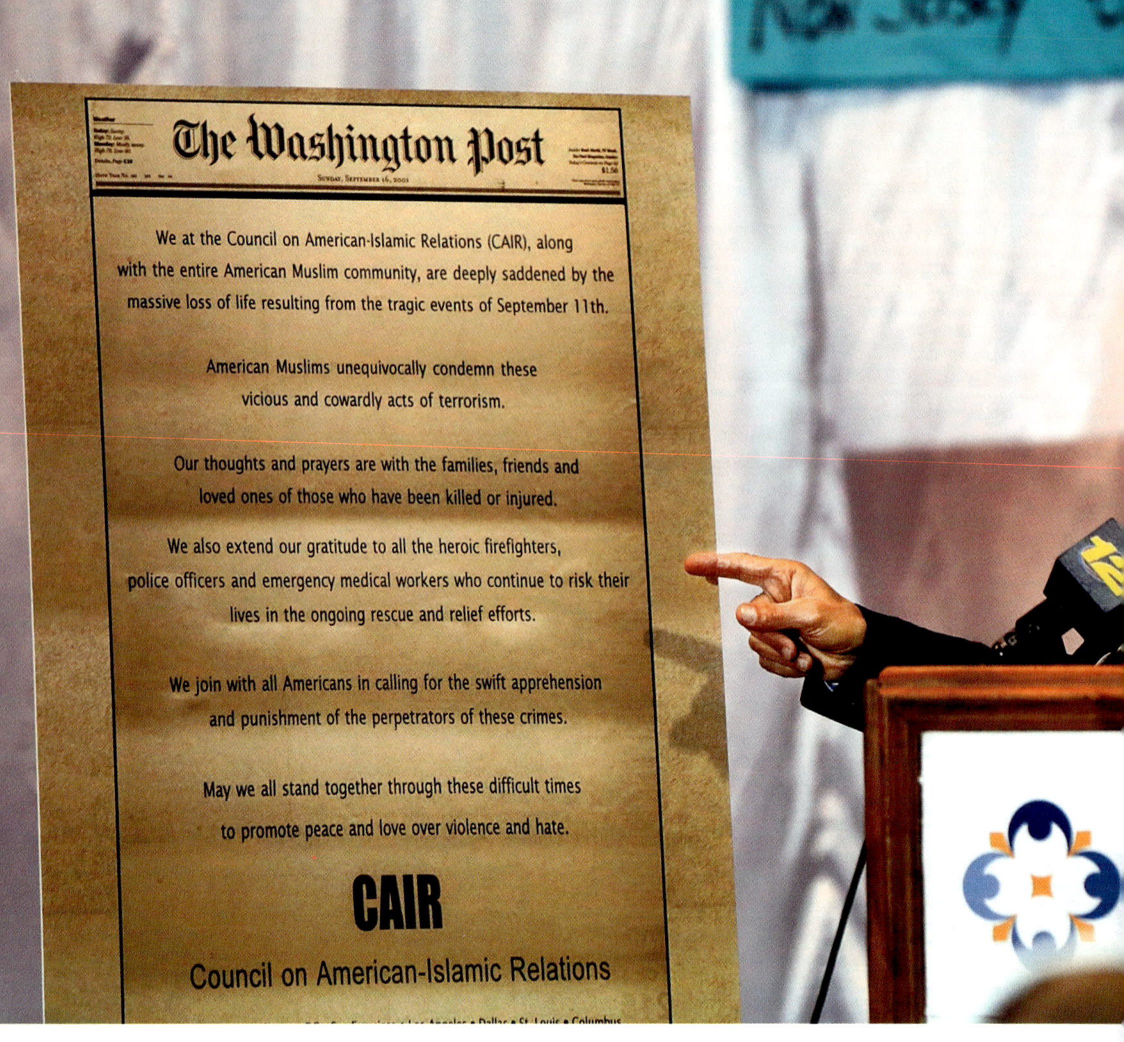

The Washington Post

Sunday, September 16, 2001

We at the Council on American-Islamic Relations (CAIR), along with the entire American Muslim community, are deeply saddened by the massive loss of life resulting from the tragic events of September 11th.

American Muslims unequivocally condemn these vicious and cowardly acts of terrorism.

Our thoughts and prayers are with the families, friends and loved ones of those who have been killed or injured.

We also extend our gratitude to all the heroic firefighters, police officers and emergency medical workers who continue to risk their lives in the ongoing rescue and relief efforts.

We join with all Americans in calling for the swift apprehension and punishment of the perpetrators of these crimes.

May we all stand together through these difficult times to promote peace and love over violence and hate.

CAIR

Council on American-Islamic Relations

On September 16, 2001, the *Washington Post* ran a statement from CAIR condemning the September 11 attacks.

Education and advocacy are also important to Anan Hafez. He was a baby on September 11, 2001. But the event still affected his life. He was teased in school for being Muslim. He saw hate crimes committed against his friends. His parents encouraged him to educate others. "My dad always told me to portray my religion and my culture with honesty and courage," Hafez said.

"I had to educate my peers because, for many of them, I was the first Muslim they encountered." He got involved in politics to fight for positive change. "A lot of Muslim Americans are much more open about countering Islamophobia, which is our legacy," he said. "Our generation, that of young Muslim Americans raised in the shadow of 9/11, was born to take on these issues."

THINK ABOUT IT

- In 2001, Facebook, Instagram, X, and other social media platforms had not been created yet. Many people did not even have cell phones. News spread primarily on the TV and radio. How do you think the lack of social media changed the way people received information about and reacted to the attacks?
- People found many ways to help one another after 9/11. Some opened their homes and prepared meals, while others donated blood or joined rescue efforts. Have you ever had the chance to help someone in need? What are steps you could take to help people in your community?
- Vigils are common after tragedies. Why do you think that is?

GLOSSARY

advocate (ADD-vuh-kayt): To advocate for someone or something is to support and promote it. Ruwa Romman wanted to advocate for her Muslim community after she faced bullying for her faith.

civil rights (SIH-vuhl RITES): Civil rights are rights given to people by a government, including protection from discrimination. CAIR fights for the civil rights of Muslim Americans.

condemned (kun-DEMD): When someone has condemned something, he has declared it to be wrong or evil. President Bush and the director of the FBI condemned attacks against Muslim Americans.

discrimination (diss-crim-ih-NAY-shun): Discrimination is treating some people worse than others for unfair reasons. Discrimination against Muslims increased after the September 11 attacks.

hijacked (HY-jakt): When something has been hijacked, it has been taken over by force. Terrorists hijacked four airplanes on September 11, 2001.

Islamophobia (iz-lah-muh-FOH-bee-uh): Islamophobia is the unfair fear and bad treatment of Islam and Muslims. Many Muslim Americans experienced Islamophobia after September 11, 2001.

marginalized (MAR-juh-nuh-lyzd): Marginalized people are excluded from the majority group. Qasim Rashid became a lawyer to help Muslims and other marginalized communities.

slur (SLUR): A slur is a hateful and offensive word against a person or group. Qasim Rashid knew life would be different after 9/11 when he heard a coworker use an anti-Muslim slur.

terrorists (TAYR-ur-ists): Terrorists are people who commit violent acts to make people feel fear or terror. Terrorists from al-Qaeda were behind the September 11 attacks.

vigils (VIH-juhlz): Vigils are events where people stay quietly in one space, usually to wait, pray, or remember. People around the United States organized vigils after the September 11 attacks.

SELECTED BIBLIOGRAPHY

Kozlevcar, Olivia. "Red Cross Volunteers Who Helped America Heal After 9/11 Continue to Deliver Hope." *American Red Cross*, 9 Sept. 2022, redcross.org. Accessed 1 Dec. 2023.

Mineo, Liz. "Born to Take On Islamophobia." *The Harvard Gazette*, 9 Sept. 2021, news.harvard.edu/gazette. Accessed 1 Dec. 2023.

Tretter, Alison. "'Lend a Hand, Do What You Can': Remembering the Generosity of Gander." *9/11 Memorial Blog*, n.d., 911memorial.org. Accessed 1 Dec. 2023.

FIND OUT MORE

BOOKS

Bah, Adama. *Accused: My Story of Injustice*. New York, NY: Norton, 2021.

Burgan, Michael. *George W. Bush: Our 43rd President*. Parker, CO: The Child's World, 2021.

Rea, Amy C. *First Responders on 9/11*. Parker, CO: The Child's World, 2025.

WEBSITES

Visit our website for links about coming together on 9/11:
childsworld.com/links

Note to Parents, Caregivers, Teachers, and Librarians: We routinely verify our web links to make sure they are safe and active sites. So encourage your readers to check them out!

INDEX